OFFENSIVE STRUCTURAL REALISM AND RUSSIAN EXPANSION IN THE ARCTIC

Mr. Brandon C. Halaychik, MA

Dedicated to Alexander Ilin, and the students of the Moscow Finance and Law University English Club, who are the future diplomats in preserving peace between two great nations.

© Copyright 2020 by Brandon C. Halaychik

Dark Raven Media
111 E. Clifford Ave.
Suite 482
Eustis, FL 32727
info@dark-raven.org

All rights reserved. No part of the contents of this book may be reproduced or transmitted in any form or by any means without the permission in writing from the author.

ISBN: 978-1653246359
ISBN: 1653246359
Library of Congress Control Number: 2020900271

Printed in the United States of America

First Edition

ABSTRACT

The Russian Federations drive to reestablish itself as a global power has severe security implications for the United States, its Arctic neighbors, and the North Atlantic Treaty Organization as a whole. The former Commander of United States Naval Forces Europe Admiral Mark Ferguson noted that the re-militarization of Russian security policy in the Arctic is one of the most significant developments in the twenty-first century adding that Russia is creating an *"Arc of steel from the Arctic to the Mediterranean."* Although the Russian Federation postulates its expansion into the Arctic is for purely economic means, the reality of the military hardware being placed in the region by the Russians tells otherwise. Implementation of military hardware such as anti-air defenses is contrary to the stipulated purposes of the Russian Government in the region. Therefore is the Russian Federation building strategic military bases in the Arctic to challenge the United States hegemony due to the mistreatment against the Russians by the United States and NATO after the collapse of the Soviet Union, or is it merely creating a buffer zone to counter what it perceives as encroachment on its security periphery by the West?

TABLE OF CONTENTS

CHAPTER	PAGE
COPYRIGHT	2
ABSTRACT	3
TABLE OF CONTENTS	4
1. INTRODUCTION	5
2. LITERATURE REVIEW	10
3. RESEARCH METHODOLOGY	19
4. FINDINGS AND ANALYSIS	24
5. CONCLUSIONS	30
LIST OF REFERENCES	34

CHAPTER 1: INTRODUCTION

Overview

The Russian Federation has attempted to reestablish itself as a global power since the collapse of the Soviet Union in the early 1990's. Under the presidency of Vladimir Putin, the Russian Federation is expanding its foreign policy and national security objectives to pre-Soviet designs. One such area of concern is the Arctic region, a 14.5 million square kilometer area situated at the top of the world with several states claiming territory to this strategically important zone. These states include the United States, Canada, Norway, Denmark, and the Russian Federation. Out of the five states listed, the Russian Federation lays claim to the largest portion of the Arctic accounting for 17,500 kilometers of land (Blunden 2009). This vast area holds a strategic monopoly for any state which can effectively lay claim, as it not only holds undiscovered natural gas and oil reserves, but new shipping lanes such as the Northern Sea routes across the top of Russia and the Northwest passage which allows access through the Canadian archipelago (Blunden 2009). It is therefore important for United States National Security interests to challenge claims by the Russian Federation to these areas and establish itself as the hegemonic power in the region.

According to a United States Geological Survey conducted in 2009, the Arctic region holds approximately 30% of the worlds undiscovered natural gas reserves and approximately 13% of the worlds undiscovered oil reserves, which are at a depth of 500 meters or less of water (Åtland 2009). This is a significant find for the Russian Federation as the Russian economy is 68% based on the production and sale of natural gas and oil to external clients such as China and Europe. Although the United Nations Convention on the Law of the Sea established in 1982 lays out the theoretical framework of the established rights of states bordering the Arctic, the Russian Federation leadership has continuously expressed the importance of the Arctic as a strategic resource base for Russia as it enters the twenty-first century (Ermida 2016).

As such, the Russian Security Strategy through 2020 identifies explicitly for the control of the energy resources in the Arctic and the Barents Sea that could develop into a potential source of conflict and the expressed possibility of military confrontation on the issue with other state powers (Piskunova 2010). To achieve their establishment in the region, the Russian Federation has already established several key military bases in the Arctic. These bases include Northern Clover on Kotelny Island, Arctic Trefoil in Franz Josef Land, and four additional bases located at Rogachevo, Cape Schmidt, Sredniy, and Wrangel (BBC 2017). Although the claim of these bases by the Russian Federation is to promote oil and natural gas exploration in the region, the bases hold approximately 150 military personnel and hold strategic offensive and defensive armaments such as anti-air defense units, which hold concern for the United States strategic abilities (BBC 2017).

The Russian Federations drive to reestablish itself as a global power has severe security implications for the United States, its Arctic neighbors, and the North Atlantic Treaty Organization as a whole. The former Commander of United States Naval Forces Europe Admiral Mark Ferguson noted that the remilitarization of Russian security policy in the Arctic is one of the most significant developments in the twenty-first century adding that Russia is creating an "*Arc of steel from the Arctic to the Mediterranean*" (Herbst 2016, 166). Although the Russian Federation postulates its expansion into the Arctic is for purely economic means, the reality of the military hardware being placed in the region by the Russians tells otherwise. Implementation of military hardware such as anti-air defenses is contrary to the stipulated purposes of the Russian Government in the region. Therefore is the Russian Federation building strategic military bases in the Arctic to challenge the United States hegemony due to the mistreatment against the Russians by the United States and NATO after the collapse of the Soviet Union.

CHAPTER 2: LITERATURE REVIEW

Reemergence of the Russian Bear

In Blankes *Imperial Ambitions Russia's Military Buildup*, the discussion presents the increase in Russian Military spending since the appointment of Vladimir Putin as President of the Russian Federation by Boris Yeltsin in 1999. Blank argues this military doctrine by Putin is a direct result of his annoyance with the United States after the collapse of the Soviet Union. This is in part to Putin's Cold War strategic thinking related to United States policy objectives in the region and his dissatisfaction with former Soviet leaders in dissolving the Soviet Union. Blank implies that due to this Russian strategy, since 2014, Moscow has repeatedly threatened Nordic and Baltic states, increased its intelligence penetration, and has deployed unprecedented military forces to include nuclear-capable submarined forces to challenge United States homogony in Europe and former Eastern bloc states which Russia feels is its area of influence

(Blank 2015). Blank discusses this reemergence of Russia as being a direct challenge to the United States which must be challenged to prevent the dominance of the Russian Federation and the loss of U.S. standing in the region.

A Place Denied to Russian Reestablishment

Jonathan Haslam's research, however, hypothesizes that Russian reemergence on the world stage is not directly related to Putin's understanding on Realist Theory but due to the denial of the United States to recognize the Russian Federation as a global power. Haslam makes the compelling argument that after the collapse of the Soviet Union the United States and other western powers offered assistance and promises to the Russian Federation to include bringing Russia closer to the North Atlantic Treaty Organization and not interfering in areas of Russian concern and influence such as the Baltic region (Haslam 1998). Unfortunately, these promises were not upheld and as such Haslam argues that Vladimir Putin is pushing back against the West to gain its *"place at the table"* and not specifically to challenge the United States militarily. The place at the table theory appears to be the catalyst which influenced the reemergence of Russia and its push into the Arctic.

A Fight for Democracy

Carl Greshman in *A Fight for Democracy* argues that Russian events in the Ukraine are symptomatic of Vladimir Putin's agenda in the Arctic region and if not checked by Western Powers Russia will have the upper hand in regional domination which the United States will be hard pressed in regaining. Greshamn contends the actions of Vladimir Putin are a direct result of his fear of the various uprising's that have occurred since his time in office (Greshman 2015). Greshman hypothesizes that it is because of this fear Vladimir Putin has engaged in a military buildup due to his belief that the United States orchestrated these events to overthrow legitimately elected officials that challenged United States authority in the region. Greshman cites the change in Russian military posture and the crackdown on internal dissidents during these revolutionary periods as evidence of Russian fears that the United States will utilize similar tactics to oust Putin from his seat of power. Greshman states this is the reason the Russian Federation has increased its military capabilities and is currently expanding its reach into the Arctic region to tie up United States forces and to ensure a stable platform to build defensive capabilities.

European Missile Defense

Andrew Monaghan and Keir Giles cite in their paper, *European Missile Defense and Russia*, that former President Barrack Obama's intent to deploy offensive missile capabilities in Europe as the mainstay reason the Russian Federation is acting aggressively and seeking its military establishment to Cold War levels in the Arctic. Monaghan and Giles highlight President Vladimir Putin's "vehement" objections to the planned deployment of the United States missile defense systems to Europe and that Russia promised "a response" if it occurred as the key reasons Russia is acting aggressively in Europe (Monaghan and Giles 2014). This hypothesis leads into the previously stated opinions that Putin is merely reacting to the United States aggression and posturing in the region and due to Realist tendencies, Putin is building up its strength in the region to battle a perceived threat from the United States. This is an essential theory as it explains the mindset of Putin when making decisions that could have an adverse effect on its relationship with its neighbors to the West.

Russia, China, and the Arctic

Thomas Pickering outlines Russian movements towards China and the Arctic region due to United States policy in Europe. Pickering indicates that United States policy related to the Ukraine and former Eastern-bloc states has forced Russia to look to the East and its border with China for friendly cooperation. Pickering cites the willingness of Russia to consummate an eight-year energy negotiation with China in a relatively short period as evidence that Russia and China are coopting to challenge the United States (Pickering 2014). Pickering indicates this relationship has evolved in part due to China's rise on the world stage and the floundering of United States foreign relations policies under former President Obama. Russia seizing on United States weakness has begun its expansion into the Arctic region in what Pickering describes as a combined effort between China, to challenge the United States in the Pacific region, while Russia focuses its efforts to aggravate the United States in Europe and the Arctic through the building of military bases that challenge the national security of the United States (Pickering 2014).

The Arctic Security Dilemma

Mariza Scopelliti, and Elena Conde Perez in their paper Defining Security in a Changing Arctic outline the radical changes that have been occurring over the past ten years in the Arctic. Scopelliti and Perez highlight that rapid warming in the region has resulted in the ice caps retreating and allowing for states to invade the Arctic in search of natural resources such as gas and oil that has been trapped for millions of years. The authors indicate that these new sources of energy, that have become available, have resulted in a race for resources in the region with the increase of Russian military expeditions (Scopelliti and Perez 2016). Mainly, Scopelliti and Perez indicate that because of Russia's incursion into the Ukraine as well as the Russian establishment of bases in the Arctic they are posed to control a majority of the energy resources for the European continent and can hold hostage these states to enforce its political agenda which could result in a security dilemma and lead to armed conflict (Scopelliti and Perez 2016).

Imagining the Arctic the Russian Way

Marina Winkler piggyback on Scopelliti and Perez by highlighting the current trend of natural resources is becoming available in the Arctic due to climate change in the region. Winkler, however, takes the problem a step further by focusing on the Russian Federations Eighteenth Century view that the Arctic region in all rights is their property due to the elongated border region (Winkler 2013). Winkler states that because of this Russia view, it will take steps to establish itself as the predominant force in the Arctic by continuing to place military forces in the region in hopes of thwarting off claims from other state governments such as the United States (Winkler 2013). This posture by the Russian Federation, however, destabilizes the region as it challenges not only United States dominance in the region, but also its national security objectives of becoming the predominant force (Winkler 2013). This will ultimately result in armed conflict between the Russian Federation, the United States, and other Western Powers as they attempt to claim the resources in the region.

Margaret Blunder further discusses the reestablishment of Russian Military Forces in the Arctic after an extended period of demilitarization. Blunder highlights that future military conflict in the Arctic cannot be ruled out due to the enormous economic stakes in the region and the blurring of maritime boundaries (Blunder 2009). Even though Blunder highlights that future military conflict cannot be avoided, she indicates that the situation in the Arctic is not critical regarding military security which is contradictory to the original abstract (Blunder 2009). Blunder acknowledges that although the Arctic region includes the territory of eight states to include Russia and the United States, she indicates that the region is militarily insignificant and more of an economic powerhouse (Blunder 2009). This, however, is in contradiction to several other theorists who indicate that the Arctic is both an economic and military vital region.

CHAPTER 3: RESEARCH METHODOLOGY

Methodology and Research Strategy

Much research has been devoted to both the Arctic region and the Russian Federation. However, little research exists regarding the Russian Federations motives in reestablishing bases in the Arctic or its objectives in doing so. Only until recently has information come to light showing the widespread strategic implications of such incursions into the Arctic by Russia though the research is vague and still fails to explicitly answer the question why is Russia re-establishing itself militarily in the Arctic. For instance, Kristian Atland's article for the *Norwegian Defense Research Establishment* discusses the rivalry between the Russian Northern Fleet and the oil industry but does not provide sufficient information as to the reasons behind the military buildup in the region itself. Additionally, Martina Winkler's work, *Imagining the Arctic the Russian Way*, provides a good basis for 18th-century Russian life around the Arctic border regions by again fails to properly discuss the underlining security reasons for Russian expansion in the region today.

This study will delve deeper into the underlying reasons the Russian Federation is reestablishing itself as a military threat in the Arctic region. Specifically, this study will begin with a review of the collapse of the Soviet Union in 1990 and the ramifications it had on the Russian morale. This is important as it will outline the underlying security concerns the Russian Federation feels it faces against the West and the North Atlantic Treaty Organization as a whole. Specifically, the study will show that both the United States and the North Atlantic Treaty Organization failed to follow through on guarantees it made to the Russian Federation during its rebuilding process which ultimately led to the Russian view that neither could be trusted. The study will then explore the strategic shifts the Russian Federation made to shelter itself from the West by annexing the Crimean

Peninsula and assisting with the pro-Russian revolution in the Ukraine in an attempt to destabilize Europe, re-establish itself as a player in the Region, and prevent the Ukrainian push to join NATO and have better relations with the West. In conclusion, the research will show that the Russian Federation is establishing itself in the Arctic not explicitly for the protection of its oil and gas industry but to gain a strategic, tactical advantage against the United States through the building of military bases and the deployment of both offensive and defensive weapons systems in line with Realist theory.

Realist Theory is one of the eight recognized theoretical approaches in security studies. The principal of Realist Theory is that states are in a continuous struggle to increase their capabilities in the absence of a recognized international equivalent of a state government (Williams 2013, 15). A subset of Realist Theory is Offensive Structural Realism, which states in part that states will pursue regional hegemony as the best means of staying safe in a dangerous world (Williams 2013, 27). Applied to the hypotheses that the Russian Federation is building strategic military bases in the Arctic to challenge United States hegemony due to the mistreatment against the Russians by the United States after the collapse of the Soviet Union is the logical choice to test the hypothesis. If the hypothesis is correct, it should show alignment between Offensive Structural Realism and the offensive movements made by the Russian State towards actions by the United States and NATO over a 28-year time span ending with the establishment of Arctic military bases to challenge United States hegemony in the region. This can be concluded by showing an increase in military expenditures and deployments by the Russian Federation after the United States failures to properly assist the Russian Government during its rebuilding process and the North Atlantic Treaty Organization's failure to properly integrate the Russian Federation through the Russian-NATO Council during the Balkans conflict.

CHAPTER 4: FINDINGS AND ANALYSIS

Overview

After the collapse of the Soviet Union in 1991, the United States and other Western countries mutually agreed to assist the rebuilding Russian Federation through economic assistance and by brining Russia closer to the North Atlantic Treaty Organization. As part of this rebuilding process, Russia joined the North Atlantic Cooperation Council and Partnership for Peace Program in 1991, which laid the foundation of cooperation between the West and Russia (North Atlantic Treaty Organization 2016). Part of the founding agreement between the two parties was assurances that NATO would not expand its membership to former Soviet Eastern Bloc states, however, in 1991 shortly after the establishment of the Partnership for Peace, NATO began talks with Georgia, Belarus, and the Ukraine, which were subsequently invited to join the North Atlantic Cooperation Council. The invitation offered by NATO to these former Soviet interests to join the North Atlantic Cooperation Council was a first step requirement needed to gain full membership in the alliance and a violation of the agreement against NATO expansion expressed to the Russian Federation. In 1997, the North Atlantic Treaty Organization and the Ukraine, which is an economic and strategic state for the Russian Federation, signed the Distinctive Partnership Charter establishing the NATO-Ukraine Commission (North Atlantic Treaty Organization 2016). On July 8, 1997, NATO tested the line even further when it invited the Czech Republic, Poland, and Hungary to join the alliance as well and officially leaving the door open for other Baltic republics to join NATO.

Although the Russian Federation officially protested this expansionist policy by NATO, in 2002 the North Atlantic Treaty Organization and Russia formed the NATO-Russian Council to establish an additional forum of consultation regarding security issues that both parties faced

(North Atlantic Treaty Organization 2016). However, in 1998 the disintegration of Western cooperation with the Russian Federation occurred when NATO entered the Baltic Republic of Kosovo on a self-described humanitarian disaster mission but failed to consult the Russian Federation prior to initiating the action in violation of the agreed upon stipulations of cooperation. In 2008, the Russian Federation engaged in military actions inside Georgia in response to accusations by the Georgian Government, that Russia had shot down an unmanned aerial vehicle inside their territory and a buildup of Georgian troops. Subsequently that same year NATO then suspended the NATO-Russian Council due to what it described as a disproportionate military action in Georgia and indefinably suspended the Council in 2014 due to Russian actions in the Ukraine (North Atlantic Treaty Organization 2016).

The collapse of effective communication between the Russian Federation and the North Atlantic Treaty

Organization has resulted in increased aggressive posturing by the alliance. Since the indefinite suspension of the NATO-Russian Council, NATO has increased its military presence in Eastern Europe to 40,000 military personnel, which is a dramatic increase from its 2015 levels of only 13,000 in the same region (The Heritage Foundation 2015). In addition, NATO has increased its military hardware in the region as well through the deployment of numerous Warrior armored infantry support vehicles, Royal Air Force Typhoon jets, Challenger 2 tanks, and the hand held Desert Hawk drones all designed to agitate the situation between Russia and NATO (Rawlinson and MacAskill 2016).

As a result, since 2014, the Russian Federation has taken its own steps to reinforce its positions in Europe and expansion into the Arctic region. A United States Army War College study conducted in 2015 entitled *"Project 1704: Analysis of Russian Strategy in Eastern Europe, an Appropriate U.S. Response, and the Implications for U.S.*

Landpower," cited that recent Russian actions regarding their military buildup and incursions into the Ukraine and Arctic region are a direct result of NATO offers to expand its membership to Georgia and the Ukraine (U.S. Army War College 2015). As a result, Russia has increased it troop mobilizations in Moldovia to 1,500 in addition to the Georgian and Armenia troop deployments of 5,000 soldiers (Russian Strategic Nuclear Forces). Russia has also reinforced its Baltic Fleet with nuclear capable warships carrying Iskandar-M missiles (Russian Strategic Nuclear Forces). Additionally, since 2014, the Russian Federation has been expanding its military footprint in the Arctic to strategic Cold War levels. Although the Russia Federation touts its expansion in the region is to gain a foothold on natural resources or to protect shipping routes, many of them are in locations that do not support this function. One such base, Alakurtti, is the home of the 80th Motor Rifle Brigade, but it cannot service the Northern Sea Route as claimed

(Reevell 2017). Another base located at Franz Josef Land, which is a chain of island between the Barents and Kara seas houses approximately 150 military personnel and an air defense contingent (The Telegraph 2015).

CHAPTER 5: CONCLUSIONS

Overview

After the collapse of the Soviet Union in 1991, the fledgling Russian Federation under the direction of then President Boris Yeltsin, looked towards the United States and Western states to assist in its rebuilding process and to be brought closer to Western systems such as the North Atlantic Treaty Organization. Promises and partnerships were made to include Russian membership in the North Atlantic Treaty Organization and the NATO-Russian Council which promised that Russia would be consulted regarding former Eastern bloc states prior to NATO involvement and that NATO would not expand into these areas in which Russia had a viable vested interest. This unfortunately was short lived when NATO entered into discussion of membership with the Ukraine and several other former Eastern bloc states knowing that they held a strategic interest for the Russian Federation. This resulted in an indefinite suspension of the NATO-Russian Council after Russia, feeling threated by the expansionist policies of NATO and the West, engaged in a Georgian conflict and annexed Crimea from the Ukraine.

The Russian Federation entered into these two conflicts not to engage the West into another Cold War, but to stop the West and NATO from strategically surrounding the Russian Federation from what it perceived as an old adversary reneging on promises of peace and cooperation. One could make the argument that had Russia partnered with Mexico and Canada to establish a new military partnership and that offensive and defensive military equipment was placed on there respective boarders of the United States, that the United States would act in kind to what the Russian Federation has done through its perceived interventions in Georgia and the Ukraine. From a strategic standpoint, Russia was left with no other option but to invade Georgia and assist in the destabilization and annexation of the Ukraine and

Crimea before they become members of the North Atlantic Treaty Organization and were covered under Article 5 of the treaty.

Offensive Structural Realism states that the anarchic nature of the international system is subsequently responsible for the aggressive state behavior in international politics. No finer example of this theory holds truer then what is being observed by the Russian Federation in response to the movements of NATO, the United States, and other Western countries.

It is evident then that as a result of such Western policies, the Russian Federation has had to take both offensive and defensive steps to counter the Western chess movements which has resulted in the offensive posturing of Russian strategic military forces in the Arctic region. As more and more polices which place the Russian Federation at a strategic disadvantage continued, Russia will seek to exploit more areas similar to the Arctic in an attempt to circumvent the West and protected its citizens from a perceived threat of violence. This, however, could be prevented if NATO, the United States, and the other Western allies understand the reasoning behind the aggressive military expansionist policy by Russia and reset the table by bringing them closer to Western Institutions Although it would be a hard fault battle to accomplish this mission based on the slights that have already occurred, trust could be rebuilt by the nations overtime and provide for a more stable and secure world.

REFERENCES

Arutunyan, Anna. "Is Russia Really That Authoritarian." *Foreign Policy in Focus*, January 11, 2007. Accessed January 15, 2019. http://fpif.org/is_russia_really_that_authoritarian/

Aybet, Gnlnur, Rebecca Morre, and Lawrence Freedman. NATO in Search of a Vision. 2010. Washington, US: Georgetown University Press. Accessed January 12, 2019. ProQuest ebrary.

Blank, Stephen J. 2015. "Imperial Ambitions. (cover story)." *World Affairs* 178, no. 1: 67-75. International Security & Counter Terrorism Reference Center, EBSCOhost. Accessed January 11, 2019.

Brown, Archie. 2015. Perestroika: Reform that Changed the world. British Broadcasting Corporation. Accessed January 11, 2019. http://www.bbc.com/news/world-europe-31733045

Gershman, Carl. 2015. "A Fight for Democracy" World Affairs 177, no. 6: 47-56. International Security & Counter Terrorism Reference Center, EBSCOhost. Accessed January 11, 2019.

Holbrooke, Richard, 'America: A European Power', Foreign Affairs, Mar./Apr. 1995, p. 50. Accessed January 15, 2019.

Lyne, Roderic. The Russian Challenge: Russia's Changed Outlook on the West From Convergence to Confrontation. London: Chatham House Publishing, 2015. 2-10.

Library of Congress. Revelations from the Russian Archives: Perestroika. Accessed January 12, 2019. https://www.loc.gov/exhibits/archives/pere.html.

McGwire, Michael and Michael Clarke. 2008. "NATO expansion: 'a policy error of historic importance'." *International Affairs* 84, no. 6: 1281-1301. International Security & Counter Terrorism Reference Center, EBSCOhost. Accessed January 11, 2019

North Atlantic Treaty Organization. 2019. A Comprehensive approach to crisis. Last modified September 1. Accessed February 7, 2019. http://www.nato.int/cps/en/natolive/topics_51633.htm

North Atlantic Treaty Organization "Relations with Russia." December 26, 2016. Accessed February 17, 2019. http://www.nato.int/cps/en/natolive/topics_50090.htm

North Atlantic Treaty Organization. 2016. "Relations with Ukraine." Accessed February 2, 2019. http://www.nato.int/cps/en/natolive/topics_37750.htm

Ratliff, Rebecca. "South Ossetian Separatism in Georgia." American University, May 2006. Accessed February 17, 2019. http://www1.american.edu/ted/ice/ossetia.htm

Rawlinson, Kevin and Ewen MacAskill. "UK Deploys Hundreds of Troops and Aircraft to Eastern Europe." *The Guardian*, 26 October 2016. Accessed January 25, 2019.

Siroky, D. S., Simmons, A. J., & Gvalia, G. (2017). Vodka or bourbon? foreign policy preferences toward Russia and the United States in Georgia. Foreign Policy Analysis, 13(2), 500-518. Accessed March 22, 2019. doi:http://dx.doi.org.ezproxy2.apus.edu/10.1093/fpa/orw061

Shifrinspn, Joshua R. Itzkowitz. "Russia's got a point: The U.S. broke a NATO promise." *Los Angeles Times*, May 30, 2016. Accessed February 1, 2019. http://www.latimes.com/opinion/op-ed/la-oe-shifrinson-russia-us-nato-deal--20160530-snap-story.html

The Heritage Foundation. "2015 Index of U.S. Military Strength: Europe." Accessed February 1, 2019. http://www.index.heritage.org/military/2015/chapter/op-environment/europe/

The White House. Press Conference by President Bush and Russian Federation President Putin. June 2001. Accessed March 12, 2019.

United States Army War College. 2015. "Project 1704: Analysis of Russian Strategy in Eastern Europe, an Appropriate U.S. Response, and the Implications for U.S. Landpower." Page 14.

United States Department of State. 2014. "Ukraine and Russian Sanctions." Accessed February 17, 2019. https://www.state.gov/e/eb/tfs/spi/ukrainerussia/

Williams, Paul D. 2013. Security Studies an Introduction, 2nd Ed. New York: Routledge. 17-21.

Made in the USA
Columbia, SC
18 January 2020